Violeta Cadena

Pasos

₪

Steps

Violeta Cadena

Pasos

彑

Steps

OYSTER
MOON
PRESS

BERKELEY, CALIFORNIA

Pasos / Steps
Violeta Cadena

ISBN: 978-1-387-84228-5

Additional copies of this book can be ordered from LuLu:
http://www.lulu.com

Oyster Moon Press is a non-profit, surrealist publishing co-op that
originated in Berkeley, California.

www.oystermoonpress.com

La gaviota que inclina su cabeza para echar un vistazo a las burbujas de la espuma en la orilla del océano ve a la vez la profundidad de la bóveda celeste.

The seagull that inclines its head to have a glance at the bubbles of the foam on the shore of the ocean sees at the same time the depth of the celestial vault.

Welcome to Cádiz

PRESENCE OF THE OCEAN

A geographical extension depends on spiritual forces to be transformed into a landscape and produce a feeling of closeness or estrangement, and so the ocean: we invent the landscapes.

Certain perspectives distributed in an area are sometimes determined by enigmatic considerations. So can a marine space also express intuitions of analogical kinds.

Thus, it is about acknowledging the substance of the spatial conditions of an oceanic plane, the qualities that emerge from its essence, setting aside the social framework that forms us. In this way, we can identify seemingly empty, but highly magnetized places. Their expansion in our spirit, pacifying what mentally slows us down, can lead a transition to a higher degree of consciousness: spatial relations then suggest a reciprocity with our existence.

Meditating about the sea is still an incentive thanks to our lack of words, unable as we are to give a pale reflection of such a prodigious object.

We do know that the tidal movement of the sea follows certain attractions. But the beautiful phenomenon suggests us rather something that swells, breathing like the sky, great unconscious with its slow rhythm unfolding, that advances and withdraws with its wide waves over the world.

The common place says that we are equal regarding our thirst for open spaces. It is, however, not always the case concerning the attraction for the density and the mysterious loneliness of certain vastness. But our mind can awaken to this: the ocean devoid of purpose will assist us.

And suddenly that deep surface acquires a particular tone as immeasurable salience that is activated to our benefit.

el pimpi Fantasma

Welcome to

CADIZ

CADIZ

Salty clarity; Bride of the air; Silver palace primarily filigree; Daughter of the ocean's entrails; Seductive mermaid with bare chest and scales of silver, all according to the poets.

We enter, anonymous stream, the streets of the city, displaying our eagerness for the unknown.

Our mind wakes up near the unspoken or the riddle of the centuries, and will wander freely if we so wish. So does it travel through time, carrying something impeccably mysterious. And suddenly a kind of subtle delirium enters the scene, luxuriously sketching some ancient legend, insinuating contact with lost ages.

Old stones stir up strange rumors from the past like a breeze that widens the day while other passers by drift away, blinded by words.

Maybe awe or nostalgia will invade us, marking the presence of certain sites. So can a doubt arise about our time, or a gentle light of promises between meaningless objects: the beauty of yearning shining like a black diamond.

In another *plaza*, strings of friendly looks or gentle movements can lead us to unsuspected thoughts or overwhelming moods, as by chance.

In this town of multiple feelings, our mind passes, not leaving a trace.

DOWN BELOW

Here a maze of forgotten subterranean galleries extends itself under our feet, gloomy dwelling of the local white cockroach.

Here is the underground site in the west that once raised oracles made of water.

Here an appropriate exercise is to meditate about darkness, about its weight in curiosity; it enhances a devotion for the night, symbol of duration. Here providence has the shape of a sloping spiral that facilitates the descent to the atavistic depths.

A stale inclination consecrates it, wide extension of the souls where visions appeared.

Here, the attendees used to praise the prestige of a figment. Then, it is said, the pattern of their murmurs reflected the violence of their faith.

Claridad salada; Novia del aire; Palacio de plata principalmente filigrana; Hija de las entrañas del océano; Seductora sirena de pecho desnudo y escamas de plata, todo según los poetas.

Nos adentramos, corriente anónima, en las calles de la ciudad, mostrando nuestro afán por lo desconocido. Nuestra mente se despierta cerca de lo tácito o del enigma de los siglos, y vagará libremente si así lo deseamos. Así viaja a través del tiempo, llevando algo impecablemente misterioso. Y de repente entra en escena una especie de delirio sutil, esbozando lujosamente alguna leyenda antigua, insinuando el contacto con edades perdidas.

Las piedras viejas suscitan extraños rumores del pasado como una brisa que ensancha el día mientras otros transeúntes se alejan, cegados por las palabras.

Quizás el asombro o la nostalgia nos invadan, marcando la presencia de determinados sitios. Entonces puede surgir una duda sobre nuestro tiempo, o una suave luz de promesas entre objetos sin sentido: la belleza del anhelo brillando como un diamante negro.

En otra plaza, cadenas de miradas amistosas o movimientos suaves pueden llevarnos a pensamientos inesperados o estados de ánimo abrumadores, como por casualidad. En esta ciudad de múltiples sentimientos, nuestra mente pasa sin dejar rastro.

ABAJO

Aquí se extiende bajo nuestros pies un laberinto de galerías subterráneas olvidadas, tenebrosa morada de la cucaracha blanca.

Aquí está el sitio en el oeste que una vez levantó oráculos hechos de agua. Aquí un ejercicio apropiado es meditar sobre la oscuridad, sobre su peso en la curiosidad; realza la devoción por la noche, símbolo de duración. Aquí la providencia tiene la forma de una espiral en pendiente que facilita el descenso a las profundidades atávicas.

Una inclinación rancia lo consagra, amplia extensión de las almas donde aparecieron las visiones.

Aquí, los asistentes solían alabar el prestigio de una ficción. Entonces, se dice, el patrón de sus murmullos reflejaba la violencia de su fe.

PRESENCIA DEL OCÉANO

Una extensión geográfica depende de fuerzas mentales para transformarse en paisaje y producir un sentimiento de cercanía o extrañamiento, y así el océano: inventamos los paisajes.

Ciertas perspectivas distribuidas en un área están determinadas a veces por consideraciones enigmáticas. Así, un espacio marino también puede expresar intuiciones de tipo analógico.

Así, se trata de reconocer la sustancia de las condiciones espaciales de un plano oceánico, las cualidades que emergen de su esencia, dejando de lado el entramado social que nos forma. De esta manera, podemos identificar lugares aparentemente vacíos, pero altamente magnetizados. Su expansión en nuestro espíritu, pacificando lo que mentalmente nos frena, puede dirigir una transición a un mayor grado de conciencia: las relaciones espaciales sugieren entonces una reciprocidad con nuestra existencia.

Meditar sobre el mar sigue siendo un aliciente gracias a nuestra falta de palabras, incapaces como somos de dar un pálido reflejo de un objeto tan prodigioso.

Sabemos que el movimiento de las mareas del mar sigue ciertos atractivos. Pero el hermoso fenómeno nos sugiere más bien algo que se hincha, respirando como el cielo, gran inconsciente con su ritmo lento desplegándose, que avanza y se retira con sus amplias olas sobre el mundo.

El lugar común dice que somos iguales en cuanto a nuestra sed de espacios abiertos. Sin embargo, no siempre es así con respecto a la atracción por la densidad y la misteriosa soledad de ciertas inmensidades. Pero nuestra mente puede impelirnos a ello: el océano desprovisto de propósito nos ayudará.

Y de repente esa superficie profunda adquiere un tono particular cuya prominencia inconmensurable se activa en nuestro provecho.

Monumentos

₪

Monuments

Un viejo librito sobre monumentos, junto con su descripción, desafía la imaginación del lector e invita a nuevas interpretaciones. Guardar ciertas palabras, o fragmentos de ellas o de frases y reorganizarlas, indica el curso de la acción. Así adquirirán tales monumentos nueva vida.

₪

An old booklet about monuments together with their description challenges the reader's imagination and invites to new interpretations. Saving certain given words, or fragments of them or of phrases and rearranging them indicates the course of action. So will such monuments acquire new life.

Una ciudad puede ser enfocada desde varios puntos de vista. Una ciudad es como un ser humano, con sus facetas negativas, pero con sus valores y con su lado bueno. Usted y yo podemos conocernos de antiguo y, sin embargo, a lo mejor no aprendemos mutuamente a ir descubriendo las peculiaridades del carácter, del temperamento y del genio. De la misma forma, usted y yo podemos estar residiendo durante años en una población sin que lleguemos a clasificar, con perspectiva separada, sus bellezas y sus contrastes.

A city can be approached from several points of view. A city is like a human being, with its negative facets, but also with its values and its good side. You and I may have known each other for a long time, and yet we may not learn to discover our respective peculiarities of character, temperament, and genius. In the same way, you and I can live for years in a town without getting to classify, out of differing perspectives, its beauties and its contrasts.

El viajero que entra en la ciudad, portavoz de fiebre, lleva imágenes ardientes, pidiendo justa elevación encima del relieve de los hechos. Por su apariencia pues se da cuenta de la insistencia del mar o de la pacotilla de España.

Todos sus gestos son de agradecimiento.

The traveler who enters the city, spokesman of fever, carries burning images, asking for elevation just above the relief of events. Because of his appearance, we realize the insistence of the sea or the trash of Spain.

All his gestures are of gratitude.

JAVIER

Este chaval se dedicó unos tres lustros como Príncipe del Mar a destacar predicciones.

El 4 de septiembre de 1928, entregó una comunicación estrechamente bella; está tirada en la carretera del Campo del Sur, rodando de un sitio a otro.

Las mutilaciones del tiempo ostentan sus flancos.

This guy spent about three decades as Prince of the Sea so as to highlight predictions.

On September 4, 1928, he delivered a narrowly beautiful communication. It lies thrown on the Campo del Sur street, rolling from one place to another.

The mutilations of time flaunt its flanks.

DOMINGO

La idea de hacer una sublime animación del espíritu del pueblo in-
dujo un incendio de voluntad incontrastable. Se instaló una constan-
cia negra, un colosal saco de bronce, y un saqueo de emblemas que
formó el recuerdo de las Bellas Artes. A él se deben acontecimientos
políticos en la cripta de la dignidad. Fray Domingo rodea su entrada.

The idea of making a sublime animation of the people's spirit gene-
rated a conflagration of undeniable will. A black constancy, a colossal
sack of bronze, and a looting of emblems that formed the memory of
the Fine Arts were established. Political events take place in the crypt
of dignity because of it. Friar Domingo surrounds its entrance.

J BOSCO

Este italiano logró perturbar la memoria de alumnos aprovechando una exquisita joven y menudas letras de circunstancia. Creó fervientemente en un aprendizaje espiritual magnífico mediante una revolución enteramente posible de la Cinematografía.

This Italian managed to disturb the memory of hundreds of students taking advantage of an exquisite young woman and small letters of circumstance. He fervently believed in a magnificent spiritual apprenticeship by way of a highly possible revolution in Cinematography.

CAYETANO

El pueblo gaditano, promontorio de lecciones prácticas, no llegó a cristalizar. En su alrededor apareció este hijo suyo que llevaba el bronce del renombre.

Cayetano, habiéndose hablado de operar las naciones, ganó una roca blanca completamente erigida.

Todas las obras de la Medicina deben ser gratuitas y ejecutadas con extensa caridad.

The people of Cádiz, a headland of practical lessons, did not crystallize. In its neighborhood appeared this son of hers who was carrying the bronze of fame.

Cayetano, having spoken of operating the nations, was rewarded with a fully erected white rock.

All works of Medicine must be free and performed with extensive charity.

SEGISMUNDO

Su viaje con cartera indescriptible fue como un fallecimiento. A los veinticinco años, Segismundo se detuvo a mirar alegorías de las Ciencias Sociales. Su último discurso lo pronunció con glosas bronceadas en mitad de un pequeño jardín delante de una fuente luminosa.

Su homenaje al periodismo existe; es un sillón.

His journey with an indescribable portfolio was like a demise. At the age of twenty-five, Sigismund paused to stare at metaphors of the Social Sciences. His last speech was delivered with bronzed words in the middle of a small garden before a luminous fountain.

His tribute to journalism exists; it is an armchair.

VICTORIA

Es un homenaje a la vida africana.

Al fondo, indígenas cuidando una figura de jaspe, y la mujer de Alicante que supo salirse de una tenaz lluvia. Aparece idea, afán, lujo en medio de la asistencia.

It is a tribute to African life.

In the background, indigenous people taking care of a figure of jasper, and the woman of Alicante who knew how to get out of a bad rainstorm. She appears as an idea, as eagerness, as a luxury in the midst of the public.

JOSE CELESTIS

José se conserva en un parterre por su obsesión oculta. Consiste en un trozo de vida que simula la bandera nacional con cuatro clavos. Se halla ubicado en un parque arado por un artista, estudio en volúmenes que constaría de la justa causa de las plantas.

José is conserved in a flower bed because of his hidden obsession. It consists of a piece of life that simulates the national flag with four nails, and is located in a park plowed by an artist, a study in volumes that would consist of the just cause of plants.

DE MORA

De sencillez bien trabajada, el gaditano que satisfacía sus gustos en un hospital hizo realizar numerosos actos para conmemorar la Existencia. Hombre concienzudo, ofreció costear una llamativa lápida dorada sobre la imposibilidad de encontrar una efigie del hecho de ser.

No obstante, la modestia de sus numerosas formas es inagotable.

Of well seasoned simplicity, the man from Cádiz who satisfied his tastes in a hospital had numerous acts performed to commemorate Existence. A conscientious man, he offered to pay for an ostentatious golden memorial stone about the impossibility of finding an effigy of the fact of being.

However, the modesty of its many forms is endless.

EMILIO C

*Emilio C se encargó del verbo cuadrado de la actualidad. Sus glosas
sobre la espléndida irrupción de una multitud popular en un salón del
Ayuntamiento dejan así mucho a la imaginación.*

Desapareció en el oscuro mármol de la nomenclatura política.

Emilio C took upon the square verb of actuality. His commentaries on
the splendid storming of a popular crowd in a reception room of City
Hall thus leave much to the imagination.

He disappeared into the dark marble of political nomenclature.

VIRGEN R

La Virgen R descansa en un patio benéfico. A la vista de una ca-
tástrofe, se presenta para trabajar una inscripción latina en mármol;
de rodillas, ofrece diseños de Triunfo fabricado. Con ocasión de la
revolución de septiembre de 1868, apareció como maremoto en liber-
tad. Un voto la derribó.

The Virgin R rests in a charitable courtyard. In the advent of catas-
trophe, she shows up to work a Latin inscription in marble; on her
knees, she offers designs of rigged Triumph. On the occasion of the
September 1868 revolution, she appeared as a tsunami in liberty. A
vote brought her down.

Lo imposible

₪

The Impossible

LO IMPOSIBLE

fotografías

Violeta Cadena – Olovsky

15 – 30 de abril de 2019

Cocina Jessy
Fernando de Jesús Corona
Xalapa, Veracruz, Mexico

THE IMPOSSIBLE

photographs

Violeta Cadena – Olovsky

15 – 30 April 2019

Cocina Jessy
Fernando de Jesús Corona
Xalapa, Veracruz, Mexico

Lo posible / The Possible

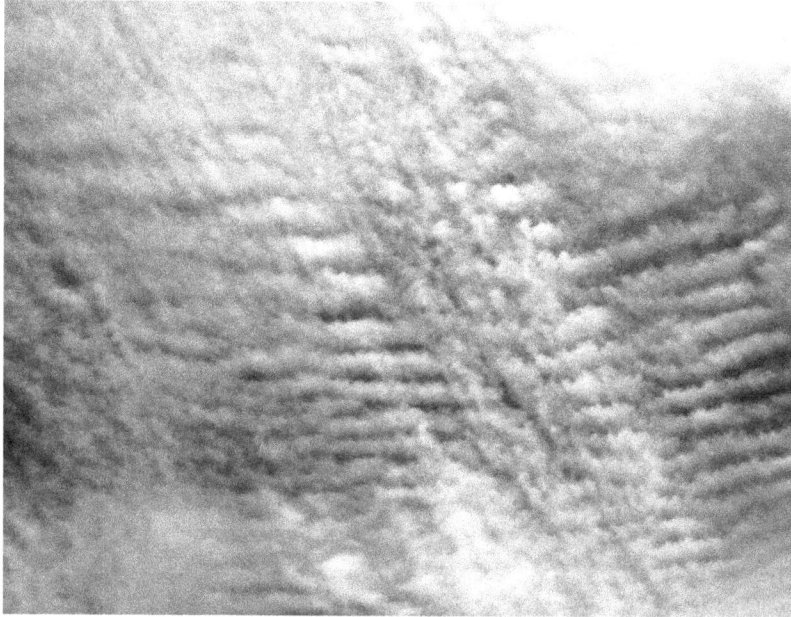

Nos envuelve el azul y al saturarnos, nos invita a vivir un ámbito que se presta al silencio.

Desde la serenidad, el azul se afirma por encima de nosotros, más que generoso.

Hay un azulamiento en el ambiente, presencia muda de la bóveda celeste. Y hasta en las calles, sentimos caminar hacia el azul de lejanía que nos inundará al final de nuestros pasos.

Ese color azulado se adentra y se cristaliza en la vida. Ya no se contenta con plasmar la atmósfera; la magnetiza hasta teñir la médula de ciertas mentes.

The blue envelops us and by saturating us, invites us to live an environment that lends itself to silence.

From the serenity, the blue affirms itself above us, more than generous.

There is a blueness in the ambience, mute presence of the celestial vault. And even in the streets, we feel ourselves moving towards the distant blue that will flood us at the end of our steps.

This bluish color forces itself and cristalizes into life. It doesn't content itself with embodying the atmosphere; It magnetizes it to the point of tinting the marrow of certain minds.

El aire

ℼ

The Air

Decrépito decir
destello de glosas
sortilegios luciendo
Entre mis dientes
como indicio
silba el aire

Decrepit saying
flash of glosses
wearing spells
Between my teeth
as an indication
whistles the air

Un eco
se despliega
inaudito
bocanada
discurso curvado
corriente de incompletud

An echo
unfolds
unheard
puff
curved speech
stream of incompleteness

Aire invocado
rumoroso
nuestro afán
fuente, sed de nada
en la luz del horizonte

Invoked air
rumorous
our yearning
source, thirst for nothing
in the light of the horizon

El levante

Respirar
el mundo
abriendo las mentes
y saber
dónde soplan

The Levante

To breathe
the world
opening the minds
and to know
where they blow

Un susurro
al cabo del día
una palabra invisible

A whisper
at the end of the day
an invisible word

Allí
donde el aire trace el día
surco verdadero
y sendas indecisas
la tarde azul
nos encarna

There
where the air traces the day
true groove
and indecisive paths
the blue afternoon
embodies us

Note: the Levante is a usually strong, very dry and hot, easterly wind
that during the summer, in the southern Atlantic coastal regions of
Spain, can be perceived as highly irritating and obtrusive by sensitive
persons.

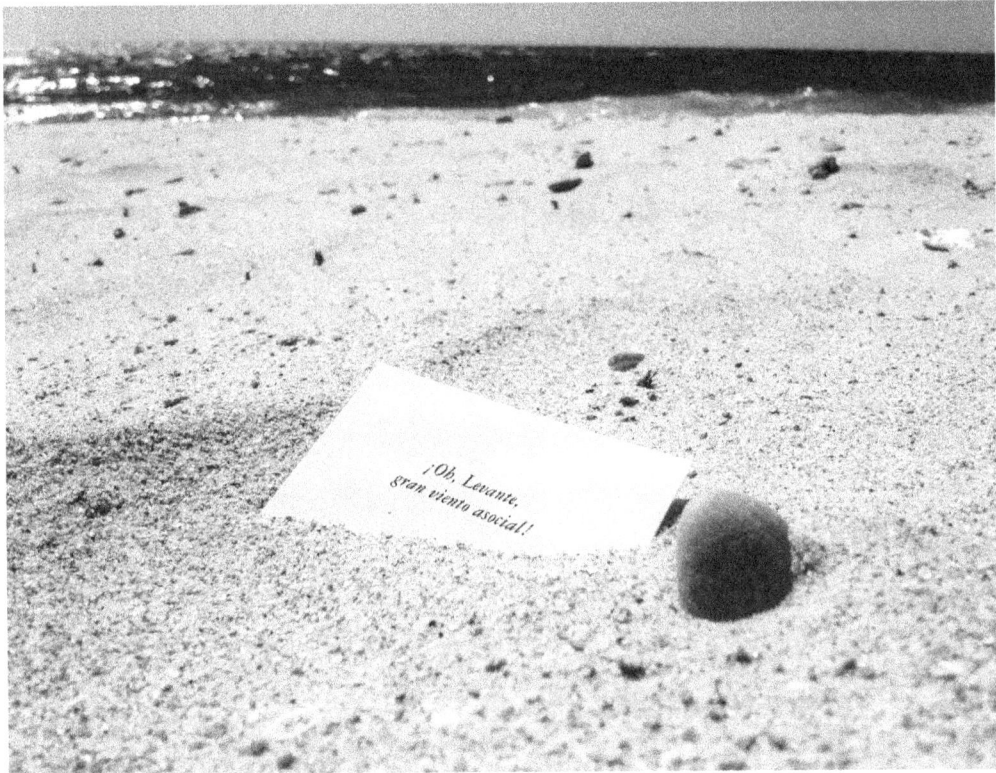

¡Oh, Levante,
gran viento asocial!

Cádiz tactilado

₪

Tactile Cádiz

(en colaboración con / in collaboration with Ruiz de Murag)

I

Abrazar una de las columnas de la entrada al Archivo Histórico Provincial, calle Cristóbal Colón.

Hug one of the entry columns to the Provincial Historical Archive, Cristóbal Colón street.

I I

Lamer el borde de la placa de mármol, calle Antonio López, número 2.

Lick the edge of the marble plate, Antonio López street, # 2.

III

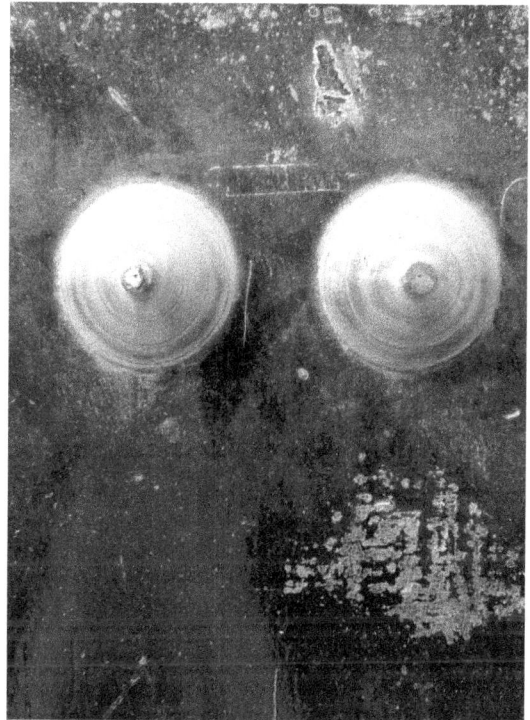

Besar los senos de bronce de la puerta del Hospital de Mujeres.

Kiss the bronze breasts on the door of the ancient Women's Hospital.

IV

Frotarse el sexo con el adorno en forma de bomba situado encima del muro del antiguo Cortijo Los Rosales y conjurar algún mal universal.

Rubb one's genitals on the bomb-shaped ornament located on top of the wall of the old Cortijo Los Rosales and conjure up some universal evil.

V

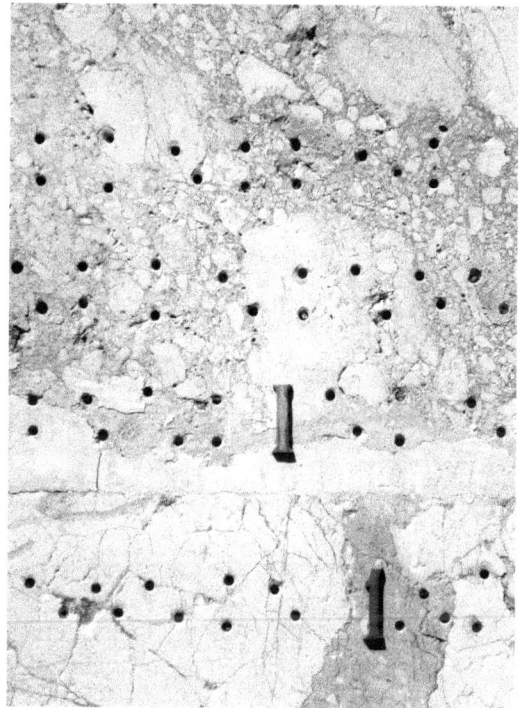

Introducir el dedo meñique empapado en aceite de oliva para descifrar el mensaje secreto de la placa de la vidente con párpado lacerado; Parque Genovés.

Insert one's pinkie soaked in olive oil to decipher the secret message of the plaque of the seer with lacerated eyelid; Genovés Park.

VI

Apoyar el rostro sobre uno de los orificios crea-
dos por el agua en alguno de los peñascos cerca
de la entrada al castillo de San Sebastián y espe-
rar el súbito chorro salado.

*Place one's face on one of the holes created by
the water in some of the cliffs near the entrance
to the San Sebastián fortress and wait for the
sudden salty jet.*

VII

Acércate a alguno del centenar de viejos cañones callejeros gaditanos, y abusa de tu imaginación.

Go to one of the hundreds of old Cadiz street corner cannons, and abuse your imagination.

Historias de pesca

₪

Fishing Tales

El ocaso

₪

The Sunset

Observa en la calle, al caer la noche, los rostros de hombres y mujeres
- qué gracia y qué dulzura revelan...
- Leonardo da Vinci

Admirable es el océano al atardecer, anónimo como sus olas o una nube tardía: fondo de promesas o de melancolía.

Salimos a pasear, presencia popular a lo largo del océano y sus insinuaciones: sombras de la ciudad que respiran su afán por el horizonte.

La mente vibra cerca de lo hablado, murmullo de los siglos, y onda como la espuma marina.

El tiempo revuelve las labores y pasa, brisa fresca en la sosegada penumbra.

Salen así los vecinos, tal vez maldiciendo su época o marcando sus memorias del lugar. Y se estira el profundo espacio mientras la gente vaga cegada por la vida o se retira sin palabras. Así se perfila una duda asumible de lo racional.

En el crepúsculo, cerca del mar, una silenciosa red de miradas distantes y de suaves movimientos llevan hacia ese libidinoso rumbo. Llevan a lo inexorablemente sublime, sólo por placer; cierta imaginación tiene tal paroxismo.

Y la hermosura de nuestros anhelos brilla, negra.

Admirable is the ocean at sunset, anonymous like its waves or a late cloud: background of promise or of melancholy.

We go out for a walk, popular presence along the ocean and its insinuations: shadows of the city that breathe their eagerness for the horizon.

The mind vibrates close to the spoken, murmur of the centuries, and waves like marine foam.

Time stirs up the labors and passes by, fresh breeze in the sedate penumbra.

So the locals come out, perhaps cursing their time or marking their memories of the place. And the deepening space is extending itself as people wander blinded by life or retreat speechless. Thus an assumable doubt of the rational arises.

In the twilight, near the sea, a silent network of distant glances and gentle movements lead towards that lustful course. They lead to the inexorably sublime, just for pleasure; a certain imagination has such a paroxysm.

And the beauty of our longings shines, black.

El parque solitario

ℼ

The Solitary Park

(Parque Genovés de noche / Genovés Park by night, Cádiz)

Y una violeta llenó
el alma de la tarde.

Como una buena muerte, sin angustia
durmíose el día, violeta mustia...
En tan propicia media luz de olvido.

And a violet filled
the soul of the evening.

Like a good death, without anguish
the day fell asleep, withered violet ...
In such auspicious half light of oblivion.

Julio Herrera y Reissig
Los parques abandonados (1902-1908)

Nos cuenta el veterano mariscador Paco Gutiérrez Calleja cómo se *pescaban* la gaviotas desde la muralla de Campo del Sur, moviendo hilos atados a piedras hasta que alguna gaviota torpe se enredaba, lo que requería mucha paciencia y destreza.

Confirma Paco que la carne de este pájaro es tierna y sabrosa. Unos la preparaban, como él, atravesándola con un hierro y cocinándola a la brasa. Según otra fuente, también se la despojaba de su piel, lavando su cuerpo con vinagre para colgarla al sol y acabar finalmente en el puchero.

Así, los pobres disfrutaban de sus exquisitos bocados -desconocidos por los ricos-, mientras al elevar el tenedor podían ver el mar, por donde giman las curiosas gaviotas.

Veteran shellfish catcher Paco Gutiérrez Calleja tells us how seagulls used to be fished from the Campo del Sur rampart, moving strings tied to stones until a clumsy seagull got tangled, which required much patience and dexterity.

Paco confirms that the meat of this bird is tender and tasty. Some prepared it, like him, by piercing it with an iron and then roasting it over an open fire. According to another source, it was stripped of its skin, washed with vinegar before hanging in the sun and then to be cooked in a pot.

Thus the poor enjoyed their exquisite taste, unknown to the rich, while raising the fork perhaps they could see the sea where the curious seagulls are groaning.

Violeta Cadena

Facebook: Violeta Cadena

OYSTER MOON PRESS

The Equestrian Turtle, by César Moro (1939). An English translation to be published in early 2022. Stay tuned for more details.....

The Last Word: Collected Poetry and Prose Volume 1 (1962-1976), by Ribitch (2019). Ribitch was a surrealist, artist, poet, photographer, and storyteller. For the first time ever his complete writings have been collected in two volumes, a project he started and his friends and family finished. This 2 volume collection encompasses 50 years of his creative expression. 372 pages.

The Last Word: Collected Poetry and Prose Volume 2 (1977-2015), by Ribitch (2019). Ribitch was a surrealist, artist, poet, photographer, and storyteller. The second of two volumes. 378 pages.

The Mountains of Mourne by Séamas Cain (2019). THE MOUNTAINS OF MOURNE is a collection of poems in English written over the course of 60 years, published in February of 2019 by Oyster Moon Press at Berkeley, California. With eight photographs by Gloria DeFilipps Brush, marking the different sections of poems. 182 pages.

Out of Odessa and Into Ideation, by Eric Bragg (2017). A collection of automatic texts and stories spanning the years 2002–2013: fully intoxicated with cunning sarcasm, social commentary and the erotic, totally "licking you with my thoughts and thinking of you with my tongue." 292 pages.

The Audiographic As Data, by Will Alexander & Carlos Lara (2016). The Audiographic As Data is none other than telepathic conundrum. It is language that renders the visible as invisible and the invisible as visible thus, transmuting both states into incalculable presence. 92 pages.

Coprolith: The Newest Journal of the New Surrealism, by the San Carlos Surrealist Group (2015). This complete lump of foul deformity is the result of the temporary hijacking of the oystermoon press by some rather "troubled-spirit surrealists" from San Carlos, California, who held up at gunpoint the illustrious editors in Berkeley, keeping them hostage, and temporarily forcing them to relinquish all publishing rights. If anyone happens to come across any copies of this thoroughly piece-o-shit book, then he or she is advised to immediately incinerate them, and focus instead on the highly esteemed volumes of *Hydrolith*. So as it were, Coprolith might for a short while have been the proverbial "turd in the punchbowl", but nevertheless by now this little problem has been fully rectified. 220 pages.

Hydrolith 2: Surrealist Research & Investigations (2014). This second issue of *Hydrolith* is a continuation of what the first volume started, which was and is to assemble a stimulating selection of exclusively recent work by groups and individuals of the international Surrealist movement, to facilitate intellectual exchange and collaboration, enabling us to concentrate the echoes of our commonalities as well as the shadows of our differences. In so doing, this volume aspires to reduce all manner of distances that exist between us. 368 pages.

Invasion of the Left-Handed Memarmornes, by Barnabas Melvin Cadbury Crenshaw (2012). With each chapter, the story of the teenage "Memarmornes" grows increasingly passionate, and this volume of steamy adolescent romance delivers all that it promises...and more. While Mr. Crenshaw's astonishingly limber voice still moves effortlessly between Peter's and Sarah's turbulent relationship and Michael Jackson's growing clairvoyance, from erotic exuberance to more interpersonal gravity, *Invasion of the Left-Handed Memarmornes* is, for the most part, a titillating book that marks the young protagonists' final initiation into the excesses and discrepancies of adulthood. 112 pages.

Mirach Speaks to His Grammatical Transparents, by Will Alexander (2011). A philosophical meditation vertically scripted. It is an extension of Alexander's first book in this mode, Towards The Primeval Lightning Field. Both books in concert, exist as a double exploration, in what, for the author, is a nascent odyssey, concerning the mind at non-limit through cellular transmogrification. 152 pages.

Carnival of Sleep, by Ribitch (2011). Between dream and hallucination, *Carnival of Sleep* opens its tent for the unwary somnambulist. Ribitch's prose and poetry are sometimes dark and humorous, sometimes sublime lamentations of erotic beauty and deeply surrealist in storytelling. They are like ruptured blood vessels, gushing forth a spray of blood droplets, each bearing a different face. Illustrations by the Author. 180 pages.

West of Pure Evil, by Josie Malinowski (2010). The labyrinthine, mercurial worlds of Josie Malinowski's *West of Pure Evil* represent a divorce between rhyme and reason, spinning off-key tales of love and pain. Sailors and whores unite to solve ancient, despicable mysteries; an act of aid brings a Fairy Kingdom to its knees; and the tragic Captain Cock is left cold and stiff by a scheming eight-year-old. These myriad poems and stories illuminate the crossover between waking and dreaming, and thereby cast an intimate, surrealist glance at the human condition. 204 pages.

Hydrolith: Surrealist Research & Investigations (2009). *Hydrolith* brings together in one volume some of the most exciting recent work from the international surrealist movement. With over 80 contributors from 17 countries around the world, the book contains drawings, paintings, games, comics, photographs, poetry, prose, theoretical and political writings on a huge variety of subjects, including special in-depth investigations of music, space and myth. The book is a must-read for anyone interested in the surrealist movement today. 240 pages.

The Exteriority Crisis (2008). In its corners, streets, gates, bars, squares, boulevards, gardens, parks and cafés, the city maintains some of the focal points of "its" unconscious. These are found and explored everyday by surrealists who obtain the essential experience of surreality in metropolitan life. The concrete experience of exteriority (which in the following collective essay we concentrate only on the city limits and beyond them) requires from us a disposition closely akin not only to the sensible renewal of people, but also to existence and its poetic reserves, and to the revitalization of the interior life that is suffering a process of sterilization because of the convulsive technologization of interiority and the progressive forgetting of life outside. 184 pages.

The Somnambulist Footprints (2008). The result of a collective project in which several contemporary surrealists and fellow travelers wrote short stories according to their own interests and imperatives, based on their common desire to subvert the very foundations of conventional reality, both on the written page and – more importantly – beyond it, in the open space of consciousness. Contributing authors: Mariela Arzadun, J. Karl Bogartte, Daniel Boyer, Eric W. Bragg, Mattias Forshage, Parry Harnden, Dale Michael Houstman, Philip Kane, Merl, Ribitch, Matthew Rounsville, Shibek, Andrew Torch, and Xtian. 216 pages.

The Midnight Blade of Sonic Honey (2008). The pairing of a surrealist novel and an automatic text by Eric W. Bragg (www.surrealcoconut.com), that were written nearly seven years apart but which tell the same story, albeit as complementary permutations of each other. Dripping with bile and centered within a gothic sensibility, this journey opens the reader's skull like a freshly cracked coconut. With illustrations by Ribitch (www.ribitch.net). 236 pages.

Oyster Moon Press is a non-profit, surrealist publishing co-op located in Berkeley, California.

If you're after individual copies, you can find our titles online at places like Lulu, Amazon, Barnes & Noble, and Borders.

If you are a bookstore, then you can make bulk orders through our distributor, Small Press Distribution (SPD) books.

WWW.OYSTERMOONPRESS.COM